AF266081

By Astor Toyos
Illustrated by Doriana Strologo
Narrated by Kikis (Sofia) Toyos
Edited by Hannah Voskuil
Designed by Diana F. Mendoza

ISBN-13:978-1979986489
ISBN-10:1979986487

Hi! My name is Sofia and I am 6 years old. I love to read and listen to stories. My favorite story is about my grandpa Gilberto, whom I call "Papi."

When Papi was a little kid, he grew up in a small town surrounded by mountains with a lot of trees. The town was called Buena Vista, and in the winter when the temperature dropped, the entire town would be all white, covered with snow.

Papi had many friends and he loved to play outside and run around the town.

Papi was the oldest of four brothers and two sisters. They all lived with their mom and dad in a small cottage made out of adobe and a corrugated iron roof. Papi shared a bedroom with his three brothers and two sisters.

Papi's family lived a simple life. Every Christmas, Papi would dream about having a Christmas tree so that Santa Claus would visit and put presents under it. They were poor, however, and they couldn't afford to buy a Christmas tree.

One Christmas Eve, Papi woke up and decided that he would go to a nearby mountain called La Elenita and chop down a Christmas tree. He was only eight years old then. Papi didn't want to go by himself and convinced his little brother, my great uncle Adolfo, who was one year younger than he was, to go along.

Papi and great uncle Adolfo spent all day looking for a nice Christmas tree, but they were not having luck finding the perfect one to chop down and carry.

Soon, it started to get late, and great uncle Adolfo became tired and cold. He tried to convince Papi to go back to their house. Papi did not want to give up. He was determined to find a Christmas tree. Great uncle Adolfo, exhausted and fed up, decided to return home by himself.

It got darker and colder. Papi was afraid of the dark and he started crying. Still, he didn't want to go home without the tree. Papi looked around. He was about to give up when Papi saw the perfect Christmas tree.

The tree was heavy and because Papi was just a young boy, he could not walk very fast. Even though he was really scared and cold, Papi was happy because he was going to surprise everyone at home with a Christmas tree.

When Papi arrived home, his brothers and two sisters were very excited to see the Christmas tree.

Papi and his three brothers and two sisters didn't have anything to decorate the tree. They decided to dig out cotton from inside one of the quilts they used to keep themselves warm at night.

The children decorated the tree to make it look like the cotton was actual snow. It looked as if it were snowing on their special Christmas tree!

That night was a happy night. Papi went to bed quite exhausted, but happy at the same time because they finally had a Christmas tree.

He could not wait for the next morning, Christmas day. After all, he had high hopes that Santa Claus would visit their Christmas tree and deliver some presents!

The next morning, Papi woke up, and in great excitement, ran to the Christmas tree. He was disappointed to see there were no presents under the tree.

Papi sat down a little sadly, thinking about this. Did Santa Claus forget? Had he been a naughty boy this year?

Papi thought about it for a bit, but soon forgot, and was happy again when his brothers and sisters woke up and started playing again with the Christmas Tree. After all, they had never had a Christmas tree before!

Hi There,
If you are one of the lucky kids Santa Claus
visits and brings special presents, please
share some of your old toys with those kids
Santa Claus could not visit, like Papi!
You will help make their Christmas special!
Cheers,
Sofia